21ST CENTURY STRATEGY NEEDS SUN TZU

The art of war is of vital importance to the state. It is a matter of life and death, a road to safety or ruin. Therefore, it is a subject that must be studied thoroughly.

—Sun Tzu
The Art of War[1]

This paper will focus on Sun Tzu whose precepts of warfare have affected, and will continue to affect, strategic decision-making today and beyond the twenty-first century. Sun Tzu's theories, as well as the theories of numerous other theorists, have a tremendous impact on warfare. His writings provide numerous ways to think through both complex and simple issues and provide advice on problem solving regarding wars and employment of military power. His principles provide military planners and strategists with a non-prescriptive approach to achieve success in warfare. Though there are many insights provided by Sun Tzu, this paper will focus primarily on his theories surrounding the importance of strategy, intelligence, deception, strategic leadership, and most importantly, achieving victory. This paper will attempt to show how some of these insights have become common language in our doctrine and will provide numerous examples of operations where commanders and strategists have successfully applied the insights to achieve victory.

Today's world is filled with uncertainty and is a world where the typical lines of the battlefield no longer exist. We live in a world where terrorism continues to grow and gain strength across the global environment, in a world where irregular warfare is common practice, and in a world where the balance of power does not appear to exist. The United States, along with its allies, are challenged globally by numerous adversaries driven by ideology, religious beliefs, wealth imbalances, resource shortages, and unlimited desires for control. According to General George W. Casey, the previous Army Chief of Staff, "the Army must be prepared to deal with a full "spectrum" of potential conflicts. For the future not only holds the danger of terrorism and the rise of failed states, but also struggles to gain control of diminishing resources —energy, food, water—made more acute by a new status quo."[2] General Casey recognized the need for a persistent campaign against extremist organizations like al Qaeda and others. All these drivers, coupled with other factors, have lead to the current strategic environment that is filled with uncertainty. Both current and future environments will increasingly require use of the Nation's military, coupled with all elements of national power to successfully address this uncertainty.

Unstable conditions have lead to increased numbers of rogue states and terrorist organizations who are willing to use any level of violence to achieve their political and ideological ends. They will continue to present tremendous challenges that will affect our role as the only modern-day superpower. In the words of a prominent national security professional, Mark McNeilly, "The United States faces many potential adversaries, both in the form of nation states and terrorist organizations. Each day, as technology progresses, the ability of these adversaries to inflict harm on U.S. military units, national infrastructure, or civilians increases."[3] In the 2010 National Security Strategy, President Obama also addressed this concern stating "moreover, as we face multiple threats—from nations, non-state actors, and failed states—we will maintain the military superiority that has secured our country, and underpinned global security, for decades."[4]

The world we confront requires a properly resourced and fully capable military with exceptional leadership, coupled with well-educated strategic planners at all levels within our government. Both military leaders and strategic planners, civilian and military, need to understand the strategic concepts found amongst both modern and historical theorists, most specifically, the tactical concepts found in the writings of Sun Tzu, which remain relevant in today's asymmetrical environment. As the former Chairman of the Joint Chiefs of Staff Colin Powell said, "I've read the Chinese classic *The Art of War* written by Sun Tzu. Sun Tzu has been studied for hundreds of years. He continues to give inspiration to soldiers and politicians. So every American soldier in the Army knows of his works. We require our soldiers to read it."[5] Sun Tzu's theories can be applied to today's environment and have been supported by leaders at all levels including those who wage war and those who have the responsibility to make the decisions about engaging in war.

As the current world superpower, the United States will continue to find itself involved in world affairs whether we choose to or not. The odds are high that the opposition we may potentially encounter will not challenge us directly with large-scale conventional warfare. Instead, the opposition will most likely challenge us indirectly and that requires an indirect approach to be applied. Sun Tzu understood this hundreds of years ago and his writings reflect so by stating, "He who knows the art of the direct and the indirect approach will be victorious."[6] He provides numerous tactical insights that can be applied from the operational to the strategic level and these insights are necessary tools to deal with both the current and the future world of uncertainty.

Sun Tzu the Master Strategist

The exact dates of Sun Tzu's birth and his death are unknown, but he lived around 500 B.C.[7] The name Sun Tzu ("Master Sun") is an honorific title bestowed upon Sun Wu, the author of the Sun Tzu Ping Fa (*The Art of War*). According to Chinese tradition, he was a member of the "Shi (intellect) during the consolidation of the Spring and Autumn Period (represented an era in Chinese History between 722 BC and 481 BC).[8] Sun Tzu's classic, *The Art of War* is the first known study of the planning and conduct of military operations. In the foreword of Samuel Griffith's, Sun Tzu, *The Art of War*, B.H. Liddell Hart, the great British strategist and thinker described Sun Tzu as the most concentrated essence of wisdom on the conduct of war, and only Clausewitz is comparable; but as theory observed, "the clarity of Sun Tzu's thought could have corrected the obscurity of Clausewitz."[9] Hart continues on stating, "among all the military thinkers of the past . . . Sun Tzu has clearer vision, more profound insight, and external freshness."[10]

Some military historians suggest that Napoleon applied Sun Tzu's philosophies in his military planning and one, Robert Cantrell, even suggested that he carried a copy of Sun Tzu's book with him on his campaigns.[11] While some historian's debate if and when a man named Sun Tzu actually existed, the great early Chinese historiographer Ssu-ma Ch'ien states that Sun Tzu was born in the state of Ch'i. Ssu-ma Ch'ien further states that he became a general for the King of Wu during the aforementioned Spring and Autumn period in China (722-481 B.C.) and won great victories for him. To hand down the wisdom he gained from his years in battle and his observations of statecraft, Sun Tzu wrote *The Art of War*. The book has given guidance to military theorists and generals throughout time. *The Art of War* became popular among not only military leaders but among leaders of the state. Cantrell went on so far as to say, "Sun Tzu's ideas cover not only warfare but state craft; not only military strategy but grand strategy."[12] Indeed, it is not too much to say that the principles found within the text of Sun Tzu's book have been used successfully in countless battles and crises throughout time, ranging from the battles of Gettysburg; to the Cuban Missile Crisis; to Operation Desert Storm; to the operations in both Iraq and Afghanistan.

Whether the knowledge found in Sun Tzu's, *The Art of War* stems from the creativity of a single mind or from the collective genius of several, matters little. What endures is the clarity of thought, the precision of expression, the proven value of the collected observation as applied to countless examples down through history. According to Mark McNeilly, "what we can all be sure of is that a book known as *The Art of War* most certainly exists and that the lessons it has to teach strategists, are as deep and meaningful today as they were two thousand years ago."[13]

Current and Projected Strategic Environment

In the parlance of the United States Army War College, the current strategic environment can best be described as volatile, uncertain, complex, and ambiguous (VUCA), with the future environment appearing to share the same characteristics, and potentially at an even greater degree. Though the United States remains the preeminent power of the world, an increasing number of state and non-state actors continue to exhibit consequential influence. This change in the distribution of power indicates a movement towards a "multi-nodal" world characterized more by shifting, interest-driven coalitions based on diplomatic, military, and economic power, than by rigid security competition between opposing blocs. Both global and regional powers are exhibiting nationalism and assertiveness that tests our partner's resilience and United States leadership.[14]

In the foreseeable future, the United States should continue to remain the foremost economic and military power though that position will continuously be challenged. The ability of the United States to maintain its position of economic and military power could be greatly affected given the enormity of the current and projected national debt.[15] New challenges will continue to surface and the world will continue to face many of the same challenges it faces today. The world population will continue to grow and become increasingly urbanized, driving the demand for already scarce resources even higher. The desire for nuclear weapons and the potential for proliferation of them by terrorists, rogue nations, and non-state actors will continue to grow.

There is growing concern as non-state actors such as criminal organizations, traffickers, and terrorist groups are working vigorously to exploit global commons by acquiring technologies to advance their interest in attempts to challenge our ability to project power from global commons. Non-state actors are using available technology to coordinate and operate globally to spread their extremist ideologies and attack the United States. These are only a few of the multitude of challenges the world will confront with the potential for armed conflict remaining an ever-serious challenge. The strategic environment today, and in the future, cannot simply be addressed with military power alone. Military power coupled with the Nation's other instruments of statecraft will continue to be absolutely necessary.[16]

During his "Landon Lecture" at Kansas State University on 26 November 2007, then Secretary of Defense Robert Gates stated "We can expect that asymmetric warfare will be the mainstay of the contemporary battlefield for some time. These conflicts will be fundamentally political in nature, and require the application of all elements of national power. Success will be less a matter of imposing one's will and more a function of shaping behavior—of friends, adversaries, and most importantly, the people in between."[17] According to Alan Stephens and Anita Baker, "many interventions in civil conflicts, failing states, and humanitarian crises, have been characterized by, and consequently suffered from, the absence of strategy."[18] Sun Tzu understood this need and addressed it accordingly through the strategy he revealed in his writings.

Significance of Theory—Sun Tzu's Strategy

Sun Tzu provides basic tools for strategist at all levels to address the complexities threaded throughout today's world of uncertainty and in one where conventional and indirect warfare tactics and techniques are required. Specifically, he brings awareness to the significance of strategy as it applies to waging war, to the concept of battle avoidance, and to the need for both military and diplomatic involvement to achieve victory. He provides a very flexible approach to address the complexities surrounding the current strategic environment that involves uncertainty, terrorism, and both irregular and asymmetrical warfare. To understand the messages embedded in his writings, several terms should be clearly understood to include, strategy, terrorism, irregular warfare. Strategy as defined in JP 1-02, is "the art and science of developing and employing instruments of national power in a synchronized and integrated fashion to achieve theater, national and/or multi-national objectives."[19]

Terrorism as defined in JP 1-02, is "the calculated use of unlawful violence or threat of unlawful violence to inculcate fear; intended to coerce or to intimidate governments or societies in the pursuit of goals that are generally political, religious, or ideological."[20] Irregular Warfare as defined in Air Force Doctrine Document 2-3, Irregular Warfare, is, "a violent struggle among state and non-state actors for legitimacy and influence over the relevant population(s). Irregular warfare favors indirect and asymmetric approaches, though it may employ the full range of military and other capacities, in order to erode an adversary's power, influence, and will."[21] A close reading of *The Art of War* shows that Sun Tzu anticipated these definitions and further, that his theory provides practical insights, strategies, and tactics that leaders and strategist have applied in past encounters, and can apply to problems in the current and future strategic environment. What Sun Tzu understood thousands of years ago, and articulated in his writing, *The Art of War*, has become common spoken language and its meanings and interpretations are threaded throughout the language of our current military doctrine.

Key Tenets of Sun Tzu

Strategy. Sun Tzu was extremely prudent as far as strategy was concerned. He considered it best to subdue the enemy's army without fighting and pointed out, "To win one hundred victories in one hundred battles is not the acme of skill. To subdue the enemy without fighting is the supreme excellence."[22] He reveals his thoughts on the significance of strategy with the admonition that "War is a matter of vital importance to the State: the province of life or death; the road to survival or ruin. It is mandatory that it be thoroughly studied."[23] Sun Tzu further states that, "Victory is the main object in war."[24] War must be studied and those involved with war planning must develop clearly

8

defined strategies to achieve success. "The supreme excellence in war is to attack the enemy's plan; next best to disrupt his alliances; next best to attack his army' the worst is to attack his cities."[25]

But, Sun Tzu did not advocate going directly to war. He understood the seriousness of war and believed that rational men had the capacity with their moral and intellectual faculties to make the right decisions.[26] More importantly, he believed that war was a last resort and that battle avoidance techniques including frustration of the enemy, the use of spies to gain information, the sowing of dissension, and the nurturing of subversion were key parts of the strategy to win.

Sun Tzu devoted considerable time and attention to concerns prior to the engaging in war to include the significance of diplomatic engagement strategies as alternatives to achieve stated objectives.[27] He expressed great awareness of the dire consequences resulting from decisions to engage in war and that diplomacy was the best means to achieve success without engaging in bloodshed as a result of fighting. He identified dire consequences that included the potential for significant draining of resources that included populations and cities. Sun Tzu believed that every possible means to avoid war should be investigated first. "Only when the enemy could not be overcome by these means was there recourse to armed force, which was to be applied so that victory was gained:

(a) in the shortest possible time

(b) at the least possible cost of lives and effort

(c) with infliction on the enemy of the fewest possible casualties."[28]

He understood and supported battle avoidance and believed those involved with the design or execution of strategy should fully understand this concept. "Thus, those skilled in war subdue the enemy's army without battle. They capture his cities without assaulting them and overthrow his state without protracted operations."[29] There are two ways this can be achieved. One is through the use of political, economic, psychological, and moral means before engaging in military efforts, and the other is through the use of a wise war strategy when military means are put into play. Wise war strategy means not just seeking to fight battles, but utilizing intelligence, deception, surprise, speed, and other methods to either outmaneuver the enemy or to ensure that any battles will end in victory.

As a result, the goal of strategy is not only to achieve the nation's aims through controlling or influencing its sphere of influence, but to do so without resorting to fighting.[30] Sun Tzu, in *The Art of War*, identified and codified many operational practices that are regarded as maxims for all types of conflicts today. He provided guidance on deception, when to advance and when to withdraw, when to attack and when to defend, the disposition of forces, discipline, and intelligence. Throughout the book, Sun Tzu stresses the significance of both the political and psychological aspects of conflict and he provides numerous observations regarding the character of war as well as the multitude of issues that a true strategist should consider when determining how to achieve victory. According to Stephens and Baker, "strategists contemplating the ends-ways-means construct at any intensity of conflict could not wish for more illuminating wisdom."[31] In the Washington Post, General (Retired) Wesley Clark cautions against the simple and sole application of military force to contemporary conflict issues, advising never go to war unless you can describe and create a more desirable end state

. . . and doing so requires a whole lot more than just the use of force. He concludes

Americans must understand that the goal of war is to achieve a specific purpose for the

nation. In this respect the military is simply a tool of statecraft, one that must work in

tandem with diplomacy, economic suasion, intelligence and other instruments of United

States power.[32]

Intelligence. Intelligence as defined in JP 3-0, Joint Operations, is "intelligence

identifies enemy capabilities, helps identify enemy and friendly centers of gravity

(COGs), projects enemy courses of action (COAs), and assists in planning friendly force

employment. The process also attempts to identify what the enemy is able to discern

about friendly forces."[33] Intelligence can also be defined as "processed, accurate

information, presented in sufficient time to enable a decision-maker to take whatever

action is required. Poor intelligence can be attributed several factors: the lack of

intelligence funding or skills; limited methods available to obtain, conduct analysis, or

the dissemination of intelligence; the inability of leadership to understand which is most

important; or the belief by political leadership the intelligence gathering is unfair or

unethical.[34] Sun Tzu repeatedly emphasizes the significance and advantages of

intelligence and drives the issue home with his focus on knowing the enemy. He

addresses why we must use all the tools available to us including imagination and

innovation to be victorious.

His attitude towards the significance of intelligence could not be more clearly

stated than in his words "Know your enemy and know yourself: in a hundred battles you

will never be in peril. When you are ignorant of the enemy but know yourself, your chances of winning or losing are equal. If ignorant of both your enemy and of yourself, you are certain in every battle to be in peril."[35] Belief that we can shape our circumstances implies ownership of a thorough and sophisticated understanding of the operating environment. Central to any understanding is access to credible intelligence—or in Sun Tzu's words, foreknowledge. According to Sun Tzu, "what is called foreknowledge cannot be elicited from spirits, not from gods, nor by analogy with past events, nor from calculations. It must be obtained from men who know the enemy situation."[36]

According to Stephens and Baker, decision makers need knowledge about ourselves, our enemies—and knowledge of our friends. It is not something as simple as projecting the future based on events of the past. Though opponents may not always know each other's intentions, they can at least understand each other's capabilities.[37] Good leaders will know their enemy's strengths and weaknesses, their preferred behavior, and how susceptible they are to deception. Most of this knowledge can only be achieved through human agents who know personally the enemy leaders they are dealing with. Sun Tzu drives the importance of this home by stating "secret operations are essential in war: upon them the army relies to make every move."[38]

According to Army General Peter Cuviello, for many years the Army had extremely limited capabilities to collect, record, store, process, and disseminate information, that is, in Sun Tzu-like terms, to know the enemy and know ourselves.[39] Commanders lacked clear situational awareness and the ability to communicate intent to subordinate leaders, which has a direct impact on a commander's ability to effectively operate. Technology is enabling us to be a transformed, network-centric military that operates in three domains—the physical domain, the information domain, and the knowledge domain. In the all-important battle for information superiority on today's battlefield, the information domain is undoubtedly the most important domain to leaders at all levels.

According to John Garstka, the assistant director for Concepts and Operations at the DOD Office for Force Transformation, "Our soldiers and equipment operate in the physical domain. The information they need is created, manipulated and shared in the informational domain. But, to succeed in network-centric warfare, we must transform our operations into the knowledge domain, where our force has the capability to develop and share high-quality situational awareness."[40] The knowledge domain is where our military has the capability to develop a shared knowledge of commander's intent and is where we have the capability to self-synchronize operations. What this means simply is that we are on the cusp of succeeding with Sun Tzu's vision to fully know our enemies and to know ourselves. Army General Peter Cuviello concludes with observation, "we use this knowledge so that we truly need not fear a hundred battles, so that we can win this war on terrorism, and so we can transform our Army to meet any challenge it faces in the 21st Century."[41]

One of the more dramatic illustrations of the connection between intelligence and strategic shaping is evident in the confrontation between the USSR and the United States during the Cold War. In this example, ignorance on the part of one protagonist of the other's capabilities might precipitate a pre-emptive nuclear strike, as a result of the unfounded fear resulting from the consequences of inaction. This sensitive perception-reaction dynamic was witnessed in the early 1960's when the Air Force and a committee reporting to President Eisenhower separately that the Soviet Union had a numerical advantage in nuclear-armed inter-continental ballistic missiles (ICBMs). The alleged "missile gap" cause tremendous concern in the United States and increased tensions between the two superpowers.

The truth was that no gap existed and that the United States actually had more ICBMs. Lack of valid information, of credible intelligence, placed leadership in the dangerous position of making decisions related to nuclear warfighting on the basis of dangerously incorrect information. High quality knowledge is critical to preventing decision makers from taking peremptory action.[42] Believing that we can shape our strategic circumstances implies a sophisticated understanding of the operating environment we find ourselves and central to any understanding is having knowledge of ourselves, of our enemies and of our friends. "As the Army maxim has it, time spent on reconnaissance, on gathering information, is never wasted."[43] Sun Tzu understood this. He repeatedly stressed the importance of intelligence and paralleled its significance with the precept of deception.

Deception. Military Deception is defined in JP 3-0, Joint Operations as "military deception includes actions executed to deliberately mislead adversary decision-makers as to friendly military capabilities, intentions, and operations, thereby causing the adversary to take specific actions (or inactions) that will contribute to the accomplishment of the friendly mission."[44] Sun Tzu's strategy of deception is highly dependent on good intelligence. Sun Tzu refers to the importance of deception for obtaining victory by stating, "All warfare is based on deception."[45] He further states, "In war, practice the art of deception and you will succeed."[46] In both of these statements,

14

Sun Tzu expresses the importance of deception in obtaining victory and he supports them by describing methods to create deceptions by using stratagem and maneuver. He provided numerous examples of how to deceive and exposes what he sees as the five qualities that are dangerous in the character of a general. Sun Tzu sees them as weaknesses and believes that by identifying and then leveraging them, leaders and strategists can develop plans to deceive and eventually defeat an opponent. The five weaknesses addressed are:

> If reckless, he can be killed; If cowardly, captured; If quick tempered you can make a fool of him; If he has too delicate a sense of honour you can calumniate him; If he is of a compassionate nature you can harass him.[47]

Leaders can select any one of these dangerous characteristics to develop deception strategies. According to Stephens and Baker, other theorists have embraced Sun Tzu's thoughts on deception with Machiavelli arguing that a flexible mind is especially important for generals and strategists, for while it may be hateful to practice fraud in life generally, in the conduct of war it is praiseworthy and glorious. Stephens and Baker further stated, "these thoughts were later found couched in more practical terms by the unpredictable Confederate commander, General T.J. Stonewall Jackson. His strategic philosophy was to always mystify, mislead, and surprise the enemy, which is exactly what Sun Tzu and others embraced."[48]

But Sun Tzu also understood that some opponents do not have such obvious and exploitable weaknesses as the aforementioned ones. For this reason, he advanced the importance of leveraging things that an opponent needs or desires in order to deceive him. According to Sun Tzu, "When able to attack, seem as if unable to attack; when using forces actively, seem inactive; when nearby, make the enemy believe you are far away; when far away, make the enemy believe you are nearby."[49] Sun Tzu believes that deception in accordance with the needs and desires of the enemy, and in accordance with what the enemy fears, plays directly into his willingness to perceive the truth. Needs and desires forecast action, and fear likewise causes action or inaction often associated with those desires. By having knowledge of your enemy's needs and desires, and by having knowledge of his fears, and when you know your enemy's weaknesses, you can leverage all of these factors to be successful in your deception plan. Deception of the enemy involves: showing the enemy what he wants to see; show the enemy what he expects to see; or have the enemy see nothing. By revealing and concealing selectively, leaders can create an elaborate strategy of overall deception.[50]

Numerous examples of successful deception operations exist throughout history. Two examples stand out. First is by looking at Soviet doctrine and the employment of deception. Throughout the Cold War the Soviets executed extensive training exercises along the West German Border in plain sight of NATO observers. This led military planners to begin believing that any Soviet attack would most likely be launched from one of those massive training exercises because it would be the only way they could move the number of divisions required to launch an attack without raising suspicion.

This doctrinal technique of deception, which the Iraqi Army was well versed in, allowed them to successfully deceive both the Kuwaiti's and others. The Iraqi Army, under the deception of a training exercise on the border of Kuwait, launched a short-lived successful invasion of Kuwait. Secondly, by looking at an example occurring during the Civil War, specifically, Pickett's Charge during the Battle of Gettysburg. After two days of intense fighting on the right and left sides of the Union line, commanding

Union generals were convinced that Confederate General Robert E. Lee would attack the center of the line.

As expected, the Confederates began shelling the center intending to destroy the Union artillery batteries in advance of troop movement. Brigadier General Henry J. Hunt, Commander of the Union artillery, wanted the Confederate General to believe they had destroyed the guns and ordered them to cease fire only to use the lull to reposition his artillery along the line in anticipation of an infantry attack.He used the time to position the guns so they could be fired directly at the approaching troops. The Confederate commanders had been deceived into seeing and hearing what they wanted and expected to see as a result of their relentless efforts. The silent guns led them to believe opportunity was on their side. Thus deception led to defeat of the attacking force of 15,000 Confederates and ultimately doomed Lee's invasion of Pennsylvania.[51]

During Desert Shield/Desert Storm, General Norman Schwarzkopf, Commander-in-Chief, Central Command (CINCCENT), understood and employed military deception as a means of gaining the advantage in order to achieve victory. "He had a superior intellect and fully understood the linkage between unified operations and the strategic goals of the coalition. Schwarzkopf's convictions included the belief that casualties could be minimized by deception and overwhelming ground force."[52] During the conduct of the war, General Schwarzkopf, for both logistical and tactical reasons, made the decision to assign United States Marine forces in a role that would keep them closer to gulf where there support was located. But, having the Marines closer to the coast also reinforced his deception efforts to convince Iraqi leaders that the coalition was planning an amphibious assault operation.[53] Sun Tzu understood and drives home the point that attacking the mind of the enemy is an indispensible preliminary to battle. He highlights the aforementioned five weaknesses in leaders and the leveraging of things that opponents need or desire as tools to cause an enemy to make mistakes, which in turn exposes him to defeat. But, along with the many tenets addressed by Sun Tzu, none appear more significant in achieving victory on the battlefield than that of leadership.

Leadership. Sun Tzu expends considerable time and energy addressing the significance of leadership and how leaders with certain competencies, characteristics, and traits, can and will lead to success on the battlefield. His thoughts are embedded in United States doctrine as articulated in Army Field Manual, FM 22-100, Army Leadership, that defines leadership as, "Leadership is influencing people—by providing purpose, direction, and motivation—while operating to accomplish the mission and improving the organization."[54] This is only one of many doctrinal tenets that address and stress the importance of leadership at all levels. Today's world of volatility, uncertainty, complexity, and ambiguity requires our senior leaders, and most importantly, our senior commanders, to have multi-level awareness and that they have conceptual, technical, and interpersonal competencies. In 2008, General George Casey, Army Chief of Staff, asserted, "Strategic leaders guide the achievement of their organizational vision within a larger enterprise by directing policy and strategy, building consensus, acquiring and allocating resources, influencing organizational culture, and shaping complex and ambiguous environments. They lead by example to build effective organizations, grow the next generation of leaders, energize subordinates, seek opportunities to advance organizational goals, and balance personal and professional demands."[55]

Sun Tzu examines the ideal character of the commander and his critical role, and acknowledges that such a leader must draw upon his experience and intuition in exercising his creative, independent judgment. He values numerous qualities that enable a commander to make rational, calculated decisions during the most demanding and difficult situations. Sun Tzu believes that steadiness, resolution, stability, patience, and calmness are critical characteristics of commanders and key to being victorious on the battlefield.[56] Many of Sun Tzu's thoughts on the ideal character of a commander can be found in Army Field Manual, FM 6-22, Army Leadership, which states "leaders motivate, inspire, and influence others to take the initiative, work towards a common purpose, accomplish critical tasks, and achieve organizational objectives. Influence is focused on compelling others to go beyond their individual interests and to work for the common good."[57]

Sun Tzu understood the significance of strong, influential leadership and believed that taking care of soldiers was a path to victory. He validates this by stating, "Thus, command them with civility and imbue them uniformly with martial ardour and it may be said that victory is certain. . . . When orders are consistently trustworthy and observed, the relationship of a commander with his troops is satisfactory."[58] Trust between leaders and commanders takes patience and energy to establish. Supporting Sun Tzu's thoughts on leadership, Mark McNeilly states, "The Art of War recognizes that successful military leadership is based on character, that to lead and command properly, one must have certain traits and values."[59] Leaders with these unique quality and caliber are hard to find and are desirable because they choose to put the needs of the nation before their own and have strong, well-developed characters.[60]

But choosing the correct commanders according to Sun Tzu may be the most important decision made by our political leaders. Sun Tzu believes the choice of the military commander must be made with great caution because of the "greater professional independence and the professionally independent position and discretionary power he would grant the military on the battlefield."[61] He states, "now the general is the protector of the state. If this protection is all embracing, the state will surely be strong; if defective, the state will certainly be weak. . . . A sovereign who obtains the right person prospers. One who fails to so will be ruined."[62] Sun Tzu continues stating, ". . . The wrong person cannot be appointed to command."[63] Decisions surrounding the choice of commanders are difficult and absolute care must be used to ensure our soldiers and civilians are lead by competent, honest, moral, and ethically strong individuals. Strategy, intelligence, deception, and leadership are four of many key tenets presented by Sun Tzu and are critical to achieving one of the most important tenets—that of victory.

Victory. Battle avoidance is a key tenet of Sun Tzu. But, according to him, once a nation decides to go to war then, "Victory is the main object in war."[64] But to Sun Tzu, victory does not necessarily mean engaging in battle. Sun Tzu drives the battle avoidance concept hard and provides strategist and leaders with a means to achieve victory through use of intelligence, through deception, by knowing your enemy, and mostly importantly, through avoidance without actually confronting him. His primary goal is to defeat the enemy without fighting. Sun Tzu states, "For to win one hundred victories in one hundred battles is not the acme of skill. To subdue the enemy without fighting is the acme of skill."[65] Sun Tzu stresses that accurate and timely intelligence of the enemy can be critical to being victorious before a battle even begins.

He understands that victory is the main object in war once the decision to go to war has been made but also understands that ". . . a victorious army wins its victories before seeking battle."[66] Each situation that commanders, leaders, and strategist confront requires careful analysis. If achieving victory requires engagement in battle, then Sun Tzu provides numerous tools for consideration. He clearly favored using means other than actual combat to win battles when those means produced the ends for which combat would have taken place.[67] Achieving victory is very clear in his writings and Sun Tzu could not be more clear about battle avoidance than through his statement "Thus, those skilled in war subdue the enemy's army without battle. They capture his cities without assaulting them and overthrow his state without protracted operations."[68]

Conclusion

Sun Tzu's theories are as valid and necessary today as they were hundreds of years ago when he wrote about strategy. Though he did not invent the principles, he observed them, used them in accordance with Chinese history, and then presented them in a way that made sense to his followers and continue make sense to leaders and strategists today.[69] His war theories are not prescriptive in nature but provide strategic planners, political leaders, and commanders a multitude of ideas and perspectives to consider when making difficult decision. In today's, and the future strategic environment, rather than planning for large-scale military operations, or even small wars limited to specific nation-states, strategic planners should develop strategies to tackle unconventional threats from both state and non-state actors who might seek to attack U.S. interest.

Asymmetric threats are not new and strategist's have been studying and addressing them for many years. General George W. Casey, the previous Army Chief of Staff, gives an excellent perspective on the current and future strategic environment by stating, "we are locked today in a war against a global extremist network that is fixed on defeating the United States and destroying our way of life. . . . This foe will not go away, nor will he give up easily. And the next decade is likely to be one of persistent conflict. We are engaged in a long war."[70]

In every era, from the pre-modern to the present day, weaker forces utilize surprise, technology, innovative tactics, or what some might consider outright violations of military etiquette to challenge the strong. Sun Tzu carefully crafts and presents numerous tactics to address asymmetrical warfare. His writings provide a guide for strategic planners and leaders, covering the many different levels and spectrums of war. When our Nation makes the decision to go to war, victory must be the objective, but victory does not necessarily mean engaging in battle. Sun Tzu drives the battle avoidance concept hard and provides strategist and leaders with a means to achieve victory through use of intelligence, deception, by knowing you enemy, and mostly through avoidance without actually confronting the enemy.

Strategic planners involved with development of war plans at all levels within government need to carefully study this thought process as opposed to engaging in potential protracted wars. They need to carefully consider Sun Tzu's recommendation stating that, "when the Army engages in a protracted campaign, the resources of the state will be sacrificed. For there has never been a protracted war from which a country has benefited."[71] When the decision is made to engage in war, then all of the tools found in the writing's of Sun Tzu need to be considered. The tools of deception, intelligence, knowledge of the enemy, speed, and diplomacy will be critical to achieving victory.

The enemy we confront today, and in the future, will continue to require leaders and strategists at all levels that have tremendous ingenuity, flexibility, and adaptability. They will continue to address a multitude of security challenges including transnational and regional terrorism, proliferation of nuclear weapons, challenges of rising powers, and all these things being underpinned by fiscal constraint.[72] According to Stephens and Baker, "regardless of the circumstances, the true strategist will always take into account four factors when analyzing a situation and before deciding on a course of action. The first is that the strategy is concerned with how to win; the second is that winning is a relative concept; the third is that strategy should not be constrained by environmental boundaries; and the fourth is that if the objective is legal, moral and realistic, and if the means match the ends, then the strategy is likely to look after itself."[73]

Sun Tzu's military thinking is only one of many different approaches to strategy but is one that both political and military leaders and strategists can learn tremendously from. The future begs many questions, but with the United States maintaining the title as the world's dominant power, the understanding and employment of Sun Tzu's strategic lessons are more important than ever before. Sun Tzu's strategic concepts emerged thousands of years ago and yet retain a compelling logic for today's political and military leaders.

Many operational practices regarded as maxims for all kinds of conflicts were first identified and codified in "The Art of War", including guidance on intelligence, deception, and strategy. "As might be expected of someone who was a practitioner as well as a theorist of warfare, Sun Tzu presented a great deal of wise advice on such matters as terrain, weather, logistics, economics, maneuver, and the application of force."[74] His concepts continue to deserve careful dissection and historical analysis. The 21st Century needs Sun Tzu's theories to address the current and future challenges facing our Nation.

Endnotes

[1] Samuel B. Griffith, "Foreword by B.H. Liddell Hart," in *Sun Tzu: The Art of War* (Oxford, NY: Oxford University Press, Inc., 2004), 63.

[2] Jeff Shear, Miller-McCune, Smart Journalism, Real Solutions, April 29 2011, "*War on Terror Promises Era of Persistent Conflict*" available at http://www.miller-mccune.com/culture/war-on-terror-promises-era-of-persistent-conflict-30653/, (accessed 17 September 2011).

[3] Mark McNeilly, *Sun Tzu and the Art of Modern Warfare* (New York, NY: Oxford University Press, 2003), 187.

[4] Barrack Obama, *National Security Strategy*, (Washington, DC: The White House, May 2010), presidential opening memo.

[5] "*Who is Sun Tzu*," 2011, available at the Sun Tzu Strategy site, http://www.suntzu1.com/content/who_is_sun_tzu/, (accessed 15 September 2011).

[6] Griffith, *Sun Tzu: The Art of War,* 106.

[7] General Tao Hanzhang, "*Sun Tzu's Art of War*", (Sterling Publishing Company, New York, 1987), 5.

[8] Mr. Li-Sheng Arthur Kuo, "*Sun Tzu's War Theory in the Twenty-First Century*, USAWC Class of 2007, pg 2.

[9] Griffith, *Sun Tzu: The Art of War*, v-vi.

[10] Ibid., v.

[11] Robert L. Cantrell, "*Understanding Sun Tzu on the Art of War*," (Arlington Virginia, Center for Advantage, 2003), 4.

[12] Ibid., 5.

[13] Mark McNeilly, *Sun Tzu and the Art of Modern Warfare* (New York, NY: Oxford University Press, 2003), 4-5.

[14] DoD, *The National Military Strategy of the United States of America*, (Washington, DC: the Department of Defense, 2011), 2.

[15] DoD, *Sustaining U.S. Global Leadership: Priorities for the 21st Century Defense*, (Washington, DD: The Department of Defense, 2012).

[16] DoD, *The National Military Strategy of the United States of America*, (Washington, DC: the Department of Defense, 2011), 2-5.

[17] Robert M. Gates, Address at Landon Lecture Kansas State University, November 26, 2007. *"Beyond Guns and Steel: Reviving the non-military Instruments of American Power,"* available at http://www.defense.gov/speeches/speech.aspx?speechid=1199, (accessed 12 September 2011).

[18] Alan Stephens and Nicola Baker, *"Making Sense of War: Strategy for the 21st Century,"* (Cambridge University Press, 2006), 247.

[19] Joint Staff J-7, Joint Publication 1-02, *Department of Defense Dictionary and Associated Terms*, (Washington, DC, Department of Defense, November 8, 2010), 327.

[20] Ibid., 346.

[21] U.S. Department of the Air Force, *Irregular Warfare, Air Force Doctrine Document 2-3*, (Washington, DC: US Department of the Air Force, August 1, 2007), 1.

[22] Griffith, *Sun Tzu: The Art of War*, 77.

[23] Ibid., 63.

[24] Ibid., 73.

[25] Ibid., 78.

[26] Ibid., 39.

[27] Michael I. Handel, *Sun Tzu and Clausewitz Compared*, (Strategic Studies Institute, U.S. Army War College), 9.

[28] Griffith, *Sun Tzu: The Art of War*, 39.

[29] Ibid., 79.

[30] McNeilly, *Sun Tzu and the Art of Modern Warfare*, 19.

[31] Stephens and Baker, *"Making Sense of War: Strategy for the 21st Century,"* 28.

[32] Wesley Clark, *"The Next War,"* Washington Post, September 16, 2007, available at http://www.washingtonpost.com/wp-dyn/content/article/2007/09/14/AR2007091401973.html, (accessed September 18, 2007).

[33] Joint Staff J-7, *Joint Publication 3-0, Joint Operations*, (Washington, DC, Department of Defense, November 8, 2010), III-20.

[34] McNeilly, *Sun Tzu and the Art of Modern Warfare*, 70.

[35] Griffith, *Sun Tzu: The Art of War*, 84.

[36] Ibid., 145.

[37] Stephens and Baker, *"Making Sense of War: Strategy for the 21st Century,"* 117.

[38] Griffith, *Sun Tzu: The Art of War*, 149.

[39] Army Chief Information War/G6, LTG Peter Cuviello, *"Army on Cusp of Sun Tzu's Dream,"* available at http://proquest.umi.com/pqdlink?index=2&did=125507401&srchMode=3&sid=2&Fmt=3&Clientid=20167&RQT=309&VName=PQD, (accessed 3 December 2011).

[40] Army Chief Information War/G6, LTG Peter Cuviello, *"Army on Cusp of Sun Tzu's Dream,"* available at http://proquest.umi.com/pqdlink?index=2&did=125507401&srchMode=3&sid=2&Fmt=3&Clientid=20167&RQT=309&VName=PQD, (accessed 3 December 2011).

[41] Army Chief Information War/G6, LTG Peter Cuviello *"Army on Cusp of Sun Tzu's Dream,"* available at http://proquest.umi.com/pqdlink?index=2&did=125507401&srchMode=3&sid=2&Fmt=3&Clientid=20167&RQT=309&VName=PQD, (accessed 3 December 2011).

[42] Stephens and Baker, *"Making Sense of War: Strategy for the 21st Century,"* 117.

[43] Stephens and Baker, *"Making Sense of War: Strategy for the 21st Century"*, 116.

[44] Joint Staff J-7, Joint Publication 3-0, Joint Operations, (Washington, DC, Department of Defense, November 8, 2010), III-18.

[45] Griffith, *Sun Tzu: The Art of War*, 66.

[46] Cantrell, *Understanding Sun Tzu on the Art of War*, 29.

[47] Griffith, *Sun Tzu: The Art of War*, 114-115.

[48] Stephens and Baker, *"Making Sense of War: Strategy for the 21st Century"*, 31.

[49] Cantrell, *Understanding Sun Tzu on the Art of War*, 32.

[50] Ibid., 33.

[51] Ibid., 33-34.

[52] Department of Military Strategy, Planning, and Operations, "*Case Studies in Joint Functions*, (United States Army War College, AY 2012), 24.

[53] Department of Military Strategy, Planning, and Operations, "*Case Studies in Joint Functions*, (United States Army War College, AY 2012), 45.

[54] U.S. Department of the Army, *Army Leadership*, Field Manual 22-100, (Washington DC: U.S. Department of the Army, August 15, 2010), 1-4.

[55] Colonel (Ret) Stephen J. Gerras, Ph.D., *Strategic Leadership Primer, 3rd Edition*, (United States Army War College, 2010), 2.

[56] Michael L. Handel, *Sun Tzu & Clausewitz Compared*, (USAWC Strategic Studies Institute, 1991), 63.

[57] U.S. Department of the Army, *Army Leadership*, Field Manual 6-22, (Washington DC: U.S. Department of the Army, October 12, 2006), A-2.

[58] Griffith, *Sun Tzu: The Art of War*, 123.

[59] McNeilly, *Sun Tzu and the Art of Moderrn Warfare*, 156.

[60] Ibid., 156.

[61] Michael L. Handel, *Sun Tzu & Clausewitz Compared*, 61.

[62] Griffith, *Sun Tzu: The Art of War*, 81.

[63] Ibid., 82.

[64] Ibid., 73.

[65] Ibid., 77.

[66] Griffith, *Sun Tzu: The Art of War*, 87.

[67] Cantrell, *Understanding Sun Tzu on the Art of War,* 23.

[68] Ibid., 79.

[69] Ibid., 60.

[70] U.S. Department of the Army, *Military Guide to Terrorism in the Twenty-First Century,* U.S. Army Training and Doctrine Command, TRADOC G2, Handbook No.1, (Washington DC: U.S. Department of the Army, August 15, 2007), 4-1.

[71] Griffith, *Sun Tzu: The Art of War*, 73.

[72] U.S Army Chief of Staff, General Ray Odierno, *Initial Thoughts - Chief of Staff, U.S. Army*," 2011, available at http://usacac.army.mil/CAC2/Repository/11-09-7CSAInitialThoughts.pdf, (accessed 16 September 2011).

[73] Stephens and Baker, *Making Sense of War: Strategy for the 21st Century,* 33.

[74] Ibid., 28.